Small Knots

Small Knots

Kelli Russell Agodon

Poems by Kelli Russell Agodon

Cherry Grove Collections

Peter —
Thank you so much for your
support & kind words. You are such an
incredible poet, so kind i giving.
I feel so fortunate to be one of
the FB chapbook poets i am so glad
to know you. Continue your wise
& lovely poems, I am looking forward
to Book 2! Continued success i
happiness to you.   all the best!
warmly, Kelli

22 July '04

Published by Cherry Grove Collections
P.O. Box 541106
Cincinnati, OH 45254-1106

ISBN: 1932339272
LCCN: 2003112222

Poetry Editor: Kevin Walzer
Business Editor: Lori Jareo

Typeset in Charter ITC BT and Zapfino by WordTech
Communications LLC, Cincinnati, OH

Cover painting: "Turning Knot," Nancy Canyon Dirmeyer

Visit us on the web at www.cherry-grove.com
Visit the author's website at www.agodon.com

Acknowledgments

Thank you to the editors of the following publications, in which these poems first appeared, sometimes in slightly different form:

"56 Knots": *Calyx, A Journal of Art & Literature by Women*, Winter 1999/2000

"A Mermaid Questions God": *Rain Dog* (UK), 2003

"After My Last Chemo Appointment, I Steal Page Six from 'The Children's Illustrated Book of Bible Stories'": *Literary Salt*, 2002

"After These Things": *Geography*, chapbook by Floating Bridge Press, 2003

"After Hearing a Woman Say the Heart is the Same Size as an Apple, and "To My Once-Ninja After His Wedding": *The Alsop Review*.

"Before the Pumpkin Reappears": *The Poet's Canvas,* 2004

"Eve Becomes the Apple Tree": *Geography*, chapbook by Floating Bridge Press, 2003

"Every day the alarm sounds": *The Poet's Canvas,* 2004

"Geography": *Calyx, A Journal of Art & Literature by Women*, Winter 1999/2000

"Fog": *Sea of Voices, Isle of Story: A WIWA Anthology of the Best Contemporary Writing*, Triple Tree Press, 2003

"Herbs For the Dead": *Crab Creek Review*, Summer/Autumn, 1999

"It's easy to wake up in someone's poem": *Three Candles*, 2002

"The Meaning of Figs": *Literary Salt*, 2002

"Mission Bell": *Geography*, chapbook by Floating Bridge Press, 2003

"Neruda's Hat": *Pontoon #6, An Anthology of Washington State Poets*, Floating Bridge Press 2003

"New Hips": *Zuzu's Petals #20*, 2002

"Not Necessarily Cancer": *Geography*, chapbook by Floating Bridge Press, 2003

"Of a Forgetful Sea": *North American Review*, 2003; and *Poets Against the War Anthology* edited by Sam Hamill, Nation Books, 2003

"Of Moths and Oil": *Samsara Quarterly*, Autumn, 2001

"On the Last Days Before His Death, My Father Returns to the Ocean": *Between the Lines,* 2002

"Pablo Neruda Lemons": *Rattapallax*, 2002

"Post-Valentine's Day with Waitress": *DMQ Review*, 2002

"Recovery": *River Oak Review*, Issue 20, 2003

"Routine Check-Up": *Branches Quarterly*, April 2003

"Sailing Lepidoptera": *The Adirondack Review*, 2002

"Sculpture": *Geography*, chapbook by Floating Bridge Press, 2003

"*Spiacente* from Rome": *Can We Have Our Ball Back*, Issue 13, 2002

"Snapshot of a Lump": *River Oak Review*, Issue 20, 2003

"Vacationing with Sylvia Plath": *Spindrift*, 2000

"Venice": *Pontoon #3: An Anthology of Washington State Poets*, Floating Bridge Press, 1999

"What I Told the Ceiling": *Geography*, chapbook by Floating Bridge Press, 2003

"What Passes By": *The Poet's Canvas,* 2004

"What the Wind Brings": *Geography*, chapbook by Floating Bridge Press, 2003

"When Women Die, Waxwings Appear": *Geography*, chapbook by Floating Bridge Press, 2003

"The Bones She Keeps" is dedicated to Nancy Canyon.

"The Meaning of Figs" is dedicated to Paula Gardiner and Melanie Noel.

"Of a Forgetful Sea" is dedicated to Delaney K. Agodon.

"Seaside" is dedicated to Rosendo M. Agodon.

"To My Once-Ninja After His Wedding" is dedicated to Howard and Karen Hu.

The poems in the section *Stitch* are dedicated to the women who have had survived breast cancer and the ones we carry in our hearts.

Creation of this work was made possible in part through a grant from Artist Trust.

Many thanks and appreciation to *Artist Trust & Soapstone: Women's Writing Retreat* for their support of the author's work from the beginning.

artist‖TRUST
SUPPORTING ART AT ITS SOURCE

The author wishes to thank the following people for their support and friendship: Bert & Gloria Baker, Alice J. Mason, Susie Cramer, Dale & Janice Cramer, Paula Gardiner, Ann Batchelor Hursey, the Mercer Street Poets, Annette Spaulding-Convy, Nancy Canyon, Tamara Kaye Sellman, Janet Norman Knox, Jeannine Hall Gailey, John Davis, Janis Loken, Jenifer Lawrence, Ronda Broatch, Marian McDonald, Jennifer Culkin, Martha Silano, Linda Bierds, John Willson & the poets at Camp Yeomalt. Also a personal note of thanks to her husband and daughter for their love & encouragement, unquestioning.

To the golden threads in my life

Delaney K. Agodon
Rosendo M. Agodon
Gloria Russell Baker

☙

And in memory of my father

Gale A. Russell
(5/14/26–9/15/92)

Something is very gently,
invisibly, silently,
pulling at me—

Denise Levertov, "The Thread"

Table of Contents

Tangle

Interweave

Stitch

Tangle

The History of _____

I.
There is not enough history in the past—
my great-great-grandmother traded England

for a new coast, birthed seven children, then
became a side note, a misspelling on an ancestry chart.

Let's talk about her son the physician, her other son
a captain under Andrew Jackson. The daughters

are named, but no one kept records of their birthdays.
Random notes fill the margins: *died young, married a farmer.*

I search through files of nothing—
Maiden name: *missing.* Place of birth: *not found.*

II.
Do not write "breast" in the Bible, Gail. And when I explain
it was the type of cancer Aunt Mattie died from: *No.*

There are certain facts we don't need to document.
Women ailed of stomach cancer, not ovarian.

Each mother existed without her body. The page of deaths
is full of question marks and when we know

what really happened, we leave that out too.
Anna Eliza, Sara Beth, Cora Lee, what were your stories?

Aunt Mattie's name is dishonestly quiet.
She didn't talk about it, and the book was shut.

III.
Somewhere in these papers kept within the family
Bible, you can see the word *slaves*

crossed out and the word *workers* penciled in.
The family says it was the way of the times,

the South did things like that. I listen to crickets
sing and wonder aloud if it's the same song

our "workers" heard in the field at dusk. *Don't focus
on the negative, dear.* The sun turns the sky pale,

back to the years we don't remember, the blank wall, white
stairs leading up to, then falling off the edge of this home.

Fifty-Six Knots

I can count the women in my family
between the wooden beads of my rosary.
They are the small knots, the tightness,
          the holding—
the ones embracing the fragility of sons
and fathers between their soft bodies,
and the lives they watch leave them.

I can count the number of prayers
spoken by men at the dinner table,
disguised as promises
          they slip out the backdoor
even before the apple cobbler
has been removed from the oven,
the smell still hot in the hands of the burned.

I can count the number of nights I have
listened to Hail Marys bleeding
from the walls, and how many times I have
          wanted to break the chain
sending the fifty-five beads scattering
like the families who prayed to them.
I imagine collection plates around the world

filling with broken rosaries, imperfect
virgins escaping beneath stained-glass skies.
In the whispering corner of the church
          a *suffered* woman unties
each knot, the sound of beads baptizing
the marble floors, the sound of women
leaving the church hand in hand in hand.

Sailing Lepidoptera

All morning we'd been discussing death.

I checked the field guide to know
it was the Spicebush Swallowtail that landed
in my hair and not the Mourning Cloak.
Maybe I'm superstitious,

but it was the same day I learned about families
in Ireland, their sweaters patterned to identify
sons and husbands—each unique stitch—in case
they drowned, a map of where to send the body.

We passed a garden of calla lilies.

The Mourning Cloak rested, wings
the color of storms, yellow lining the edges
of waves, blue crescent moons
sailing to the rim.

And I wondered if this is what the fishermen saw,

the ones who were pulled under—ocean
moving forward, slice of moon to the East,
bubbles of breath pulling upward
where sun should have been.

Fog

      settles like sheets of insulation slipping
            from between wooden boards.
The sky, tired of living above us
      drifts down, puts its fingers in the ocean,
            lingers with waves and tugboats.

An entire island has been covered,
      we have thrown a sheet over the sofa
          to keep dust from settling
in homes of the dead.

Each morning, the ferry sounds
      searching haze for small boats,
          for fisherman dreaming of mermaids
they left back on shore.

Of Moths and Oil

We know the ocean
was painted black that day.
We curled up in the bottom
of a continent and hoped
the waves flowed north.
Every time I think
I know pain, I remember the fire
I watched burn on the edge of a city
and I hurt again.

There were two boys there, playing
by the stream. We believed
no one could become the brilliant
sunrise, the same glow that birds
return to each spring.
So we slept in, despite an open
window, the small leak underground,
notes carried in beaks.

Where did the moths flutter that morning:
I saw them in the trees, hoping
(if moths can hope) to vanish into the bark.
And if they can hope and vanish,
maybe we can too, like wings hitting the glass.
My bedroom window
never rests when the moon is out,
calling paper into the sky,
taking night out of the ocean.

Vacationing with Sylvia Plath

Maybe I should have come alone.

Maybe if the clouds didn't resemble
tombstones and I had brought something
more upbeat to read
the ocean wouldn't seem so final—
an ongoing thought carried to shore
then taken away,
washing the same green sock
over and over again.

Maybe if I was taking medication
or at least St. John's Wort,
maybe if I had a chocolate bar
to eat between breakdowns
the seagull's cry would be more of a sigh
and the waves wouldn't seem so blue.

Maybe a lot of things. Maybe
if I could slip into Sylvia's mind,
sort out the spices in her spice rack,
alphabetize them and dust them off.
Maybe then I'd understand how
it's the little things that pull you under.

It's easy to wake up in someone's poem,

the way prodigies awake in paintings
of sunflowers and lily ponds.

But we do not wear the skin of geniuses,
sometimes I lose the checkbook for days

or the note with the phone message
I jotted down while eating egg rice,

using head and eye gestures
to tell my daughter not to slide pennies

into the CD player, to take
the Venetian beads off the cat.

These are my daily poems, life falling
around me on scrap paper—my sister cries

because her new English cottage is without
its antique lightning rod, my other sister

gleeful her doublewide came furnished.
God sets us in boats and pushes us onto the lake

of perspective. It's easy to ignore the narrator
while she rests on shore in her white flannel robe,

forgetting we will wake from the page,
that our tuxedos are only black ink, white paper.

New Hips

These are softer than the ones I wore
before she grew inside me.

These are chambray, washed so many times
you can feel the stitching coming apart

in your hands. I will not send them back.
I will not try to repair their shape. Now,

they curve with the universe,
with that faint line on the edge of oceans.

Those tight and narrow memories
held in photographs have left me

still cutting the waves as I dove in.
These new hips open doors to whitecaps,

pull the moon a little closer, reconnect
the constellations, which had just become stars.

Of a Forgetful Sea

Sometimes, I forget the sun
sinking into ocean.

Desert is only a handful of sand
held by my daughter.

In her palm,
she holds small creatures,
tracks an ant, a flea
moving over each grain.

She brings them to places
she thinks are safe:

an island of driftwood,
the knot of a blackberry bush,
a continent of grass.

Fire ants carried on sticks,
potato bugs scooped
into the crease of a newspaper.

She tries to help them
before the patterns of tides
reach their lives.

She knows about families
who fold together like hands,
a horizon of tanks moving forward.

Here war is only newsprint.

How easy it is not to think about it

as we sleep beneath our quiet sky,
slip ourselves into foam, neglectful
waves appearing endless.

A Mermaid Questions God

As a girl, she hated the grain of anything
on her fins. Now she is part fire ant, part centipede.
Where dunes stretch into pathways, arteries appear.
Her blood pressure is temperature plus wind speed.

Where religion is a thousand miles of coastline,
she is familiar with moon size, with tide changes.
She wears the cream of waves like a vestment,
knows undertow is imaginary, not something to pray to.

Now her questions involve fairytales, begin
in a garden and lead to hands painted on a chapel's ceiling.
She wants to hold the ribbon grass, the shadow of angles
across the shore. She steals a Bible from the Seahorse Inn;

she will trust it only if it floats.

On the Last Days Before His Death, My Father Returns to the Ocean

When he wakes,
he wants to suck ice chips,
slip beneath the morning news,
become the crossword puzzle for a while.
No longer does he drop crab pots
at the end of the dock, children
following like young fishermen.
These days his world is an aquarium,
the same three fish circling.
He looks up from his coffee
and nods to the window
as if he can see the ocean
over his reading glasses.

How I Lost My Father's Suit

Its fabric tattooed my skin, stitched lines
across my fingers, but I couldn't hold

the last knot

of breath he let go of.
I kept quiet in the hospital

when the nurse
iced his eyes, rechecked
his organ donor card.

Family scattered
around the second floor—

waiting room, gift shop,
the cafe where they served
minestrone soup, his favorite

daughter disappearing
into the parking lot,
the most beautiful

day in September,

a pocket of holes,
a list of his medications,

a copy of the receipt for his eyes, blue
sky unable to compete with the shadows,
long threads dangling from the seams.

The Bones She Keeps

When we look at the teeth
we guess coyote, not dog.

And this?
The shoulder blade of a seal,
or perhaps, a river otter.

There is a bone on every windowsill.

What about this: A cat: A skunk?
I see part of a jawbone in the white
curve she holds in her palm,
the spine of a raccoon.

And when we line them up,
this white alphabet of what's left,
a new species is born across the table.

I mention the cow skull I found
on a Mexican highway,
how I brought it back
to my apartment, dropped it
in a bucket of bleach,

only to watch black legs emerge,
the widow exiting an eye socket.

Even now, I can't think of bone
without remembering the spider,
how the living always make room
in the spaces the dead leave behind.

Herbs for the Dead

There are certain ones they keep—
my grandmother's chamomile hair,
my father's rosemary tattoo,
the dill feathers in the hat of my Aunt Jackie
growing taller with each month she is beyond.
But some they like to give away,
like the feverfew that grows two graves down,
Eliza Mulberry wears small
daisy-like flowers sprouting from her lapel,
a baby who died at six months
has foxglove reaching towards the sky,
a dozen white rattles,
a dozen broken hearts on each lip.
I wonder if Fred Wiggins knew that one day
his headstone would peek out of purple sage,
an herb that healed so many,
now soothes the soul of his old tired grave.

A Realist's View on Grieving

In the early days of loss,
      it walks with you, tries to carry
      your bags or basket of laundry.
Notice how I say *you*, when I mean *me*.
This can be called denial, or maybe laziness.
Counselors know the right term.
They make psychosis seem normal,
      as if the bagboy at the grocery store
      also stayed in bed for weeks.
Like you did. Or I did.

This is where I change the subject,
      where I no longer respond, just listen.
Tell me again about your brother,
      the high school boy who died
      in a car accident.
I've seen photos of the tree, the telephone pole,
      metal molding itself around wood.

Now, insert another name,
      change *car accident* to *cancer*.
Rearrange the numbers on the gravestone.
It is always the same person dying
      and re-dying in someone else's life.

Place the calla lilies deep in the vase
      the earth holds with its body.
Grass touches each fingertip, the living speak:
      a crow in the madrona,
      the heavy truck on the roadway,
      the first sounds of moths
      as the sun begins to fade.

Autumn Poets

A gray-haired evening and another
burial of a friend, the neighbor
who grew dahlias like children
for a small audience of bees.
These funerals and their inconveniences
that cannot be said aloud; I whisper
them to the field of cars I pass in my black suit,
fingering the dust on the widow's Cadillac.
So forgive me when I don't ask
where you are going for the winter,
if I might have the recipe for your mint and tomato
soup. All the dates on my calendar lie
open, crumbs of flexibility, night-
practiced, and hoping not to hear from any of you
too soon.

Interweave

After Hearing a Woman Say the Heart is the Same Size as an Apple

I.
I begin to consider which one I keep in my chest.

A small pumping Fuji or Bailey Sweet.
I am part pie, part fritter, part turnover
in bed and listen to the thump thump thump of an Empire,
the whisper of Paula Red, the morning yawn of Sunrise.

II.
When I say I love you I taste cinnamon,
sugar, my coated center
beating again. Never bitter, I toss the green ones
to Adam, halve another to find a star.
O sweet apple of my—

      unpeeling, pale white
      skin appearing in your hands.

III.
My mother plucked the low ones
from trees planted the year I was born.
      Every harvest, carrying ribs
of baskets to the orchard, we gathered each heart.
Hours later my hands were red, but I continued,
nothing more than a fist opening and closing.

Post-Valentine's Day with Waitress

I looked for the crumbs of January in a poem
about snow. I chanted the words, *O terrible*

white beauty and the waitress raised her eyebrows,
tapped her pen against her wrist. She asked,

"Are you reading poetry?" the way someone
asks, "Are you wearing pants?"

The idea seemed so unusual, that I imagined
she had never undressed for anyone.

I told her that I could still remember
the lines from a poem someone sent me

one Valentine's—
When you appear all the rivers sound in my body.

She told me that sometimes she can hear the ocean
from her apartment window. She thinks

that all water tries to speak to us, even the coffee
brewing behind her on the counter.

The Next Poem

seldom satisfies. It's the poem before that you
fell for, the one whose lines you repeat

for weeks, keep going back to its page
for a quick nuzzle or maybe the whole shebang

over and over until you aren't sure if your hands
hold the book or if the poem is carrying you

to the bedroom, supporting your head as you rest
cheek against pillow. This is the poem

you don't care that everyone knows you're seeing,
the one you proudly bring to social gatherings,

heck, even to family reunions to meet your strange
Aunt Sylvia who's never liked any of your dates

and it doesn't matter since you and the poem
will run off before pie is served.

This is the poem you think about when the poet
at the mike clutches note cards, keeps mentioning

hydrangeas, the way father drank too much,
something about origami, moths or egrets.

This is the poem you wait for at bus stops,
at places you once frequented together hoping

it will drop by, say your name across a crowded
restaurant and you will turn, spill your drink

when you see it again, how you remember why
you fell for it the moment it begins to speak.

In Answer To Your Question:

"What If I Follow You Like Sun to Moon?"

You will be leaving as I arrive late
to parties dressed in night and diamonds, black
holes and the universe in my clutch.
I drink Manhattans with owls and marsupials,
howling cats on balconies become the background
music of others' dreams.

Sunrise is a synonym for *mourning,*
for pulling the shade down, turning the knob to off,
kicking my shoes under the bed and disappearing
beneath the sheets (like the Ptolemaic system
or a flat world). Now you awake, jump

into every dew-covered beginning, every pool
of creation: fingers almost touching
on a chapel ceiling, eggs becoming tadpoles, God
opening to the first page and reading how we began.
I cannot be your audience,

every morning-bird taking flight to somewhere else.
I have already moved on, I am on the other side
of you explaining astronomy—the moon revolves
around earth, not the sun—you will never catch up,
we will never touch, this room is much too big.

Living Room Explorers

Let me slip off my boot of Italy, my sweater
of Zimbabwe and map the dining room table,
the chairs, the matching ocean-colored plates.

We're a number on the earth: latitude wine,
longitude bread and trying
to become our own island. I recognize

our shadow on the wall, continent-sized,
we're Greenland on an elementary school map.
Explain Mercator.

Put your finger on the globe and find North
America. Again. You're Columbus
on my couch discovering and rediscovering

nothing and my heartbeat,
a meteor shower beneath skin,
a new love or another way to chart it.

Measure the distance between relationships
and carry me to mountaintops in the hands
of someone who never saw stars

from his city balcony, who only counted streetlights
as a boy and mistook them for stars, mistook
the sound of traffic for waves. Discover him

in the curve of your mouth, in your breath as you
ask *where,* your fingers never refolding the map,
never wanting to find the end of another evening.

Spiacente from Rome

I apologize for the weather,
for what my mother taught me not to do,
even when in desperate need
of a bathroom. I apologize for the size
of our hotel room, for the narrow staircase,
the darting cat.

I apologize at night, inch by inch
over the small of your back, your shoulder
blades, your chest. I apologize for the rib
I seem to have taken, the weeping
Virgin on the nightstand, the empty Frascati
wine bottle hidden in the tombs. More so,

I apologize for my lack of understanding,
for opening our suitcase to a man
who wasn't a security guard, leaving my ticket
in the restroom, not learning Italian
or even Spanish. Yes, you were right: *Ich haette
eine romanische Sprache lernen sollen.*

I apologize for not wearing
the right shoes, for blisters upon blisters,
for the holiness I chased or wanted. I apologize
somewhat for the hours of tourist attractions,
your windbreaker's broken zipper,
the Saint's foot you forgot to touch.

I apologize sulfur-fingered
for lighting the candle when there were already
enough burning, already enough travelers
begging for something.

You Can Never Have Too Many Rosaries

Like lilies, they seem to multiply each season.
Having slid from a Bible, find them
mixed with lingerie, wrapped around
the straps of a black bra, a rose-patterned

thong tossed across the rug. Spread them
across the photo of your mother,
use broken ones to hold back the curtains
in the kitchen, the hair from her eyes.

Carry them in your pocketbook with the snapshot
of your son, the picture of the girl who came
with the wallet and the twig of lavender
you picked from the abandoned fairground.

Remember, faith fits in the tightest pocket
of your jeans, in the cracks of your palms,
and in the fine roots of strawberry plants.
It is the song that continues to play

after the band has gone home. Worn
like a loosened necktie, let the beads hang
down your shirt, over the wine stain
like long fingers reaching for your belt.

To My Once-Ninja After His Wedding

Because of you, I again seek out the signs that
precipitate desires: shooting stars, falling objects.
—Pablo Neruda, "Love"

That night, when you knocked on my window
dressed in black, your face covered with a ski mask,
numchucks in your pocket, you told me you were out
walking, writing poetry and looking for a fight.

I was sixteen and could only offer you time,
my parents' porch, a night sky. I remember
even then you believed in math while I believed
in stars, waiting for the opportunity

to wish on anything falling. Now fifteen years
later, we watch a slideshow of your wedding,
your wife tells me that after the Columbia sparked
over Texas, the son of one of the astronauts

returned to high school only a day later searching
for normalcy. Our teenage years follow
like dusty trails and you plan your return to NASA,
rebuild another shuttle to send above us.

Constellations shift, memories drop and even
poetry is awkward in this small space, but
because of you, I again seek out the signs that
precipitate desires: shooting stars, falling objects.

What was it you said about Pablo Neruda:
You visited his home in Chile, but you didn't know
who he was until later when you wrote a letter
to your bride, quoted from one of his poems.

Neruda's Hat

On a day when weather stole every breeze,
Pablo told her he kept bits of his poems
tucked behind the band in his hat.

He opened the windows to nothing
but more heat, asked her to wander with him
down to the beach, see if their bodies
could become waves.

When they returned he placed his hat,
open to sky, in the center of the table.
She filled it with papaya, figs, searched
for scraps of poems beneath the lining.

By evening, the hat was empty
and his typewriter, full
with pages that began something about ocean,
something about fruit.

And they didn't notice the sky, full of tomorrow's
stars or the blue and white swallow
carrying paper in its beak.

They sat outside until the edge of daylight
stretched itself across a new band of morning,
a shadow of a hat washing onto the shore.

Day of the Dead

Heaven is made from cigarette wrappers
while ashes disguise the floor to hell.
Which ground shall we dance on tonight?

We move into evening, exhale
those who aren't here while others
fill our lungs like fog.

We hope to bite into skeleton,
pan de muerto, skin from the oven.
A tablecloth of lace edges

weaves beneath a ribcage,
our bodies' bare language
as breath brings us together.

We become each other's smoke,
roam around in a chest cavity,
our hearts fill with each other's fingers.

Piñata Metaphor

The heart is being beaten
by children who have only said
I love you to relatives.
They would hit it harder
if they were grown,
if there were rings and veils involved,
uncomfortable silences that last
the whole car ride home.

The heart is hanging from a pole
and they want inside it,
to rip away the lining and let it open.
I want to tell them it will be
this way for the rest of their lives.
There will always be one person
with a stick and a giant heart
suspended somewhere,

and sometimes, they'll want to hit
the heart, but miss—a blindfolded
soul with a stick, swinging and moving
in circles trying for a piece.
Other times they'll want to take the stick
and beat the person holding the heart.

The heart never breaks,
only the string holding it does.
When it falls, sometimes the small hole
hidden beneath crepe paper opens,
and all the treasure ever imagined
spills out.
Other times, it just falls.

Pablo Neruda Lemons

Some say you will fall
in love after sucking them
dry,

that if you cut through
their center, the sea will
open in your veins.

Believe me when I say they are
the tips of flames
you undress in front of,
the drip of sweat from the one
on top. You will want to be in
the hands that peel them,
to disappear
in this stranger's skin.

Before the Pumpkin Reappears

We are running away from nothing but time.
It is easier to stay inside and mop the linoleum, organize
the cleaners under the sink by fragrance, by bottle size.
How many times can we redesign the living room
in terra cotta, Southwestern rugs?

We have spent all night talking about our history
as if we haven't been telling the same stories to each other
for the last fourteen years. I've seen children who watch
a Cinderella video so many times that their eyes are small
pumpkins and their feet will fit any size shoe as long
as it's glass. So I wonder if you and I keep talking
we'll remember our fairy godmother, rewrite ourselves
back into that carriage,

into that photograph from Mexico
where we ate quesadillas with papaya, listening to
the waitress explain about New Pesos, how we wanted
to give her our bank account for not letting us get taken,
for not sending us into the streets alone.

Every day the alarm sounds

thirty minutes earlier than I expected
and I make the decision to sleep, awake
or roll over to someone I love
more than philosophy, disappear
        a few more minutes in his hands.

Too often I get up.
The mirror appreciates grogginess,
the extra minutes staring into the glass.
Is God on the other side of this image?
The shower curtain, the first gate
        to heaven:
                O soapy angels,
wings of waterdrops down our backs,
where shall we fly today?

Every thirty minutes the ferry leaves
and sometimes I am the casual pedestrian
waving at neighbors as I board,
other times I am spitfire, ferry workers
holding ropes as they see me running.
I leap—

every day arrives earlier than expected.
It's more about love than philosophy,
more about minutes than disappearing.
God is on the other side, the return trip,
the white-haired angels who wave back,
        the mirror through which we all fly.

What Passes By

Today as the older couple walks their angry dog
past my porch and the farmer who fixed
the sheep's fence three times last week,
reposts his handmade sign by the roadway:
please drive slowly when sheep are escaping,

I try to imagine life ten years from now
as a teacher had us do in high school.
Then, I guessed an island with postcard beaches,
an egret or nene on the roof of my hut, knowing
I would never check the clock, not even own one.

Now, ten years seem even closer
than a plane ride across the Pacific.
It has something to do with mortgage,
with never wanting to go inside on warm evenings,
and realizing that fifty is not as old as I thought.
Or sixty.

And maybe I look at that older couple
yanking their yapping dog close and saying,
For God's sake Max, you're ruining our walk,
the same way they said it yesterday
and the day before that and how they'll keep saying it
every day of their lives until Max disappears,
or they do, the way friends appear in obituaries
and strangers appear in our photographs.

The farmer continues to put out his sign
and the sheep continue to explore the countryside
through new openings, and some days I wake to find
a lawn full of sheep roaming my garden.
They never think about tomorrow
or where they will wander. I sit on my porch

and wave to the farmer staring at his open fence
knowing there will be a new hole tomorrow.

Trying To Decide Where To Retire

I keep thinking about Portugal, the bread cart that rolled
into town in early morning sun, but what if the bread man
is no longer and we have to shop at the store that smells
of fish where everything's deep in salt and sand?
I remember the bus that almost drove off a cliff,
how I swore I would never ride it again,
but it was the only way out of the village
except on foot or by horseback and the town donkey
looked so hot I could not ride him; I thought he was
panting. So we walked and melted into the landscape,
the yellow grass, so many orange flowers I could not
name. The bus passed us seventeen times before I waved
it down and the driver made a point to say, *You are beautiful
when you are sweating* and smiled as if I were not the woman
who earlier insisted he turn in his license to the Portuguese
government then thanked God for my life. How I loved
that view over the Atlantic where so many lucky fisherman
cast their nets catching all that was swimming, silver
and glistening as they pulled another day's work aboard.

Seaside

I will always live seaside
      with you,
even if you never learn to swim
and I have to pull you from deep water,
carry you to the beach
I will always live
      seaside with you
even while the scientists
talk earthquakes and tsunamis
I will teach you to surf
and we will ride the wave
that covers our house, even then
I will always
      live seaside with you
in a cabin or house,
tent or silver trailer
I will
      always live seaside with you
when our wheelchairs
rest in sand and
we use driftwood for canes
I
      will always live seaside with you
after our lives fold into stories
and our ashes float onto shore—
the footprints left by others
will never take us away.

Stitch

Routine Check-Up

Driving home,
I hear heartbeats in the wipers.

Has this always been here?

Rain shapes fog into patterns:
my mother's pearl rosary, a simple stitch
of my wedding gown uncoiling
before the ceremony.
Now I imagine cancer
as a cloud spreading to earth,
its threadlike veins
growing.

You're so young. I'm sure it's nothing.

Long thin fingers
slip through the window cracks.
Winter is a thief trying to enter
too soon. I remember Saint Peregrine

Let's just run a few tests.

and try to believe his prayers
exist in these raindrops,
that verses sealed in liquid
bless the madronas,
the roadway, the dunes before
my home, my body
as I walk from the garage
to collect my mail.

You do have a family history of it.

Maybe if it weren't October,
and letters arrived without that stamp—
the line-drawn woman in the corner
reaching her hand skyward,
whispering, *it might be you.*

In Search of Constellation Y

This is the beginning, the bang
of cymbals and the galaxy
expanding. Four small stars,
(I saw them) x-rayed against white
light, a universe existing
under skin.

These are the details
they look for, the cluster
of stars that grow, stretch
into a new constellation called *Stage 1
Cancer*, called *Don't-Worry-
Your-Family-Just-Yet*, called
Possibility.

This is the thin ice of ponds, the first freeze,
the wait before knowing if winter
is over or just beginning. Microcalcifications
appear like snowflakes.

It's the unbutton-my-shirt conclusion,
the tango with needles in my flesh-colored suit.
A rocket is ready to launch
through interstellar dust, the earth drifting
from view. Sunlight enters the hospital
window as the first sign to heaven. No,
it is only a star radiating daily.
Is it single, alone,
a cause for concern?

What I Told the Ceiling

I always thought my first ultrasound
would show the small hands
of my unborn child;
its jewel-sized heart beating inside me.
Instead, doctors search for a different growth,
one we don't throw parties for,
buy cigars or mail announcements
to our friends—
their unknowing lives taking place
as we wait for test results.

The monitor glows in LSD color.
The artist drunk with anger
has painted the screen scarlet—
waves, explosions, a single rib,
an apple waiting to be picked,
maybe still green, if we can find it now.
The nurse cringes slightly
and documents a mark for the radiologist.

I am ripe, I whisper to the ceiling.

She loses eye contact when I ask her
what she's found.
I want to pluck the fruit
from my body. Return the apple
to the tree, to the invisible seed
it appeared from. What am I growing?
Who can I blame?

Not Necessarily Cancer

The new cluster of cells must be the group of lost tourists
that wandered Florence when I bought a purse
from the leather-heavy man singing *God Bless American Girls*
and slipping a matching wallet in my hand just because
the shape of my wrist reminded him of his daughter's.
I was afraid to fly alone then, fourteen hours on a plane
to Europe while the world awoke and slept below me.
My life was small like the complimentary peanuts,
the packet of cheese, the tiny prayer
that came with the meal. Not yet to Italy
the pilot came over the intercom;
we were making an emergency landing in Paris.
I remember thinking that I had never seen the Eiffel Tower
or the dome of the Sacre Coeur where inside strangers knelt
after lighting candles for other strangers.

Snapshot of a Lump

I imagine Nice and topless beaches,
women smoking and reading novels in the sun.
I pretend I am comfortable undressing
in front of men who go home to their wives,
in front of women who have seen
    twenty pairs of breasts today,
in front of silent ghosts who walked
    through these same doors before me,
who hoped doctors would find it soon enough,
    that surgery, pills and chemo could save them.

Today, they target my lump
with a small round sticker, a metal capsule
embedded beneath clear plastic.
I am asked to wash off my deodorant,
wrap a lead apron around my waist,
pose for the nurse, for the white walls—
one arm resting on the mammogram machine,
that "come hither" look in my eyes.
This is my first time being photographed topless,
I tell the nurse. *Will I be the centerfold*
or just another playmate?

My breast is pressed flat—a torpedo,
a pyramid, a triangle, a rocket on this altar;
this can't be good for anyone.
Finally, the nurse, winded
from fumbling, smiles,
says, *Don't breathe or move.*
A flash and my breast is free,
but only for a moment.

In the waiting room, I sit between magazines,
an article on Venice,

66

health charts, people in white.
I pretend I am comfortable watching
other women escorted off to a side room,
where results are given with condolences.

I imagine leaving here
   with negative results and returned lives.
I imagine future trips to France,
   to novels I will write and days spent
beneath a blue and white sun umbrella,
waves washing against the shore like promises.

Sculpture

I have become the Venus de Milo.

With stone eyes, I watch doctors
gawking like tourists, gripping
their million dollar Instamatics
to photograph me from every angle—

no red velvet ropes to keep them
beyond.

Have you ever seen
the other side of a statue?
Overlooked details wait
to be discovered—

shoulder blades welcome
two hands open, palms to sky.

We forget to turn corners,
walk the same straight line for years,
and never notice patterns in the cobblestone,
the empty churches along the way.

Inside a chapel, a man sketches
the outline of a woman
onto the cover of a Bible.
She will live there for years.
She will know the fingers that trace her.
No one will know his name.

Wander behind me.
See how my shoulders lean forward,
how my hips support lead blankets,
the strength it takes to hold them up.

Recognize me from my paleness,
from the curve of my back,
from the lack of a signature and wonder
if God is ready to chisel
his name in my side,
or if his thumbprint is already pressed
into the pedestal on which I balance.

What the Wind Brings

I keep remembering the pesticides
I never washed from strawberries,

how many perfect berries I ate without asking,
How did snails avoid you?

In my garden, lettuce is a paper doily,
a lace handkerchief with detailed edges.

Nothing goes unscathed—the chard, the spinach,
each a cousin of netting, a copy

of the paper snowflake my daughter
hung beneath the mantel.

Now at the market, I pass bins of untouched lettuce,
smooth apples and cherries, boxes of holeless

strawberries grown in fields where the green
haze drifts past the cows, the small farmhouse,

the school where children die early
from lymphoma, Hodgkin's. But I can't blame

the strawberry because it may have been
the nectarine, the peach, or neither.

This is what I crawl back to, what the wind brings
from the fields, the reactor down the way,

the millions of possibilities hidden
in a dust cloud, the well water, the smog

traveling from the city like a kidnapper
working his way into the suburbs,

the escaped con driving the countryside,
searching for a new place to settle.

After These Things

The nameless red berries, the moss,
always the moss on the evergreens

and fallen logs, reminders
of all the women buried.

Some reach their fern-like arms
from blankets of soil,

while others, wearing a veil
of powder meant for gypsy moths,

lean into shadows, become the opalescent
glow, the folds in the bark.

The residue is everywhere—
on fruit and skin and future

lives questioning the landscape,
feeling the earth for a stone.

The color of death will surprise the waxwing
carrying warnings in its beak.

Tree branches are bone-white with disease,
names written on every leaf.

Eve Becomes the Apple Tree

Apples were dropping
     like heartbeats. She gathered
green ones like small birds, tried
to return them

to branches that released
     too soon, before days
could stretch into autumn, become
a wingspan of red.

Budding circles disappeared
     in long grass. The field
was an empty church and these apples,
an offering. She put on the hospital

gown of bark, slipped leaves over
     wrist bones.
One apple remained, any answers
slithered past her.

The Meaning of Figs

I place a fresh fig on my breast
after this suggestion:
it can cause the lump in your body
to become a small bruise and disappear.

Now hope blooms in a blossomless tree,
in the wasp that enters to pollinate
the flowers hidden inside this fruit.

And I wonder how many miracles seeped
from the missions they grew by,
through the ground and into their roots:

Perhaps, Demeter will return tonight, reveal
this fruit of autumn to those who don't believe
in all that can be kept in such a small space.

I wait for the bruise while Cleopatra's life is taken
by an asp hidden in a basket of these small fists,
leaves sewn like clothing, my faith
steaming in a poultice of figs.

Venice

Rusty church bells don't sound,
instead we listen to the cathedral
eroding, remains from ailing statues
dropping in the canals
pouring over—

the place where we live is unwell.

As we cross the flooded piazza,
balancing on raised boards, we remember
how we captured the city on paper,
held church between our fingertips,
lit a candle at the end of a line—

pray as the waves wash in.

Paper boats drift under these planks,
words fade in puddles,
and poems once written, return
to their original thought, a spark
of the match,

the flame forgetful of why it was lit.

Now, it seems
we all scramble through these streets,
a thousand women vanishing
into the architecture, a million more
holding us up between alleyways.

Venice is dying,

the painter said to the sky.
Set the gondolas adrift to float

between our church's doors.
Ask the gods—
how long must candles burn for the dying?

When Women Die, Waxwings Appear

By evening, the tips of their wings are dusty
from footsteps of men who don't know
what to do with themselves,

from children jumping rope
in an abandoned lot unaware
that anything has changed.

Waxwings appear in the madronas.
Someone has died and they try to carry sadness
to a bed of twigs, search for string and straw,
small branches to weave into edges.

By nightfall, the tips of their wings are arrows
for the men who don't know where to go,
for children looking for their way home.

At times, a bird will steal tissue from the hand
of a mourner, cover its nest to keep grief
from slipping back into families living below.

These days, every limb contains a nest;
there are never enough wings to hold the men
who try to comfort their children who linger
with hope of finding a new way home.

Self-Portrait in Waiting Room

I am the whole
field, the voltage on the fence
to keep the horses in. I am the face
the doctor must talk to, the sickness
he makes his living on. I am what
Shakespeare never wrote about
and did, the leaky pen, the parchment
paper, the rickety desk. I am the smallest
hole in the wood where the powder-post
beetle burrows. I am the open
tackle box, the handle that breaks.
I am the thread, needle and thimble,
the stitch never tied off. I am the growing
field, the harvest not tended. I am waiting
for the nurse, for my name to be called, for
understanding. Did I say understanding:
I meant closure.

Recovery

Shadows disguise guests
bringing balloons and flowers.
Ghosts periodically dropping by
to wish me well, rearrange the bouquets,
adjust the tint on the television.
Strangers paid to help,
dress like angels without wings,
offer juice, move the crowd
in and out like weather.

Tonight, the moonlight tries to steal
darkness from the hollow of my chest,
slips through the sheets and moves
across the room.
Morning, ready to lure night
away from corners, from the hole
against my ribs, ties knots in healing.

I try to undo death and night and dying—

when black mares run
from the edges and circle,
I send them across the valley
over hills of days and prairies
left undiscovered.
A mile perhaps, a hundred acres
of plains to ride and be forgotten.

The sun knows I am not well,
spends the morning
taking inventory of my room.
What remains on the nightstand—
a lump of bagel,
a half-sipped ginger ale,

a crossword puzzle
empty of even the easiest words.

After My Last Chemo Appointment I Steal Page Six from "The Children's Illustrated Book of Bible Stories"

Someone will not meet Noah,
at least not in this book.
I hold the flood in my pocket,
part of the story and the edge

of the rainbow from page seven.
In the picture, the sun cuts a hole
between clouds, just wide enough
for God to slip through.

And it rained . . . the words slip
from the waiting room;
I keep this scene as if it held
something beneath its waves.

Outside the clinic, I look
to the sky expecting a dove to fly
above me with its olive branch,
white wings open like hands.

But the rain begins and any hope
of birds is leaving. Somewhere
a woman is building an ark.
I know it.

Mission Bell of Haiti

The island you held in your palm,
curved and arched.

You walked the same land for years,
until the horizon quivered,

rippled against sky and white
clouds descended.

We lost track of weather;
the aging building

soon tumbled. Remember
how it stood complete.

Remind me how you loved
the mission. With most of it gone,

you look to the iron bell,
place your hand against stone,

feel the heart that still beats as strong,
though only one side remains.

Geography

I put my hand where my left breast used to be.

When she called, I didn't want to tell her,
as if speaking the word over the telephone line
would confirm it, accept it, allow it
to keep growing.
Let us forget the unsettled lava bubbling beneath.

Instead, I said,
I am a map of the world.

The oceans and continents I carry
inside, the fragile imprint of the earth
I wear on my chest—
I am the mainland now, full of prairies
and hills, canyons and valleys
spread out across my land—
the unexplored mountain
has been replaced,
craters don't keep secrets.
I am reworking my topography.

We are all volcanoes.

I heard my mother crying
on the other side of the country; her tears
could flood the small cities I carry
above my ribcage. She whispered
to the phone, "What do you look like?"

I wanted to say,
I look like the moon, beautiful and complete.
I wanted to say,
I look like a gardenia leaf, solid and firm.

I wanted to say I am lovely.

Instead,
rivers flowed down the new terrain.

Notes

"After These Things": The title of this poem was taken from Revelations 4:1.

"Autumn Poets": The title of this poem was taken from Emily Dickinson's poem "XLIX: *Besides the autumn poets sing . . .*"

"Day of the Dead": *Pan de muerto* is Spanish for "bread of the dead" and is used in the Day of the Dead festivities.

"Of Moths and Oil": is in memory of Liam Wood, 18, and the ten-year-old boys Wade King and Stephen Tsiorvas who died in the Bellingham pipeline explosion on June 10, 1999.

"Pablo Neruda Lemons": The title of this poem comes from a line in "[I am fruit crazy. I love six]" by Frances Chung.

"Post Valentine's Day With Waitress": *O terrible white beauty* is from David Lehman's poem, "January 16" and *When you appear all the rivers sound in my body* is from Pablo Neruda's poem, "The Queen."

"Sailing Lepidoptera": refers to two butterflies, Spicebush Swallowtail (*Papilio troilus*) and the Mourning Cloak (*Nymphalis antiopa*) both native to North America.

"*Spiacente* from Rome": *Spiacente* is Italian for "sorry" and *Ich haette eine romanische Sprache lernen sollen* is German for "I should have learned to speak a Romance language."